Transcript

by Adam Stutz

Transcript by Adam Stutz

Transcript

by Adam Stutz

Cooper Dillon

Acknowledgments

Deepest thanks and appreciation to the following individuals who helped me develop, edit, and organize this manuscript:

Adam Deutsch and Cooper Dillon Books for the willingness to publish this chapbook and for Adam's discerning editorship; Adam Veal for his insightful critiques; Justin Levitt for his observations and suggestions; James Meetze for his guidance, encouragement, and patience; Mark Wallace for his invaluable advice, conversation, and mentorship; Amy Bartley, Renee Anderson, Erin Sharer, ellis meridian, Benjamin C. Roy Garrett, Austin Brown, and the Louisiana Street Writer's Collective for their insightful critiques, suggestions, and willingness to meet;

My father and mother whose love instilled in me an unwavering sense of stubbornness and determination that still manages to survive, even in times of severe doubt; and,

My wife, Destinie Gardner-Stutz, who has been my guiding light, my love, and my greatest support.

Sincere thanks and gratitude are expressed to the editors of the following journals in which some of these poems first appeared, sometimes in different versions:

Prelude: "THE HUM"; "APOLOGY;" *The Equalizer*. Second Series: "RECITAL," "ECHOES;" *A Sharp Piece of Awesome:* "THE LOVELY RESIDUES;" *The Cultural Society:* "SLEEPER."

Transcript
Copyright © 2017 by Adam Stutz
All rights reserved
First edition
Cooper Dillon Books
San Diego, California
CooperDillon.com
Cover Art & Design: Jesse Caverly, for Excelsior & Smith

ISBN-10: 0-943899-02-9
ISBN-13: 978-1-943899-02-9

Printed in the United States

Table of Contents

ECHOES	1
APOLOGY	3
CAVEATS	5
SHELL	6
THE EDGE OF IT	8
PLANES	10
SLEEPER	11
EXIT SONG	13
LEAVING CONVENIENCE	15
COMEDIAN	17
RECITAL	19
ARITHMETIC	20
BOXES	21
THE HUM	23
THE LOVELY RESIDUES	28

ECHOES

Too many chorales—

        cacophonies—

constant companions

        insisting upon

reverb conversations,

        chants in anger,

                broken promises.

A storm drain,

        a drain pipe,

                a pipe organ

                      calling—

persistent, bodiless choirs

vibrating inside

        the morning's

                open throat,

swelling

        into a chorus,

                nothing,

into a crescendo,
                    nowhere.

APOLOGY

Smashed persimmons

           misgivings

slipped/ broken open/

laid down &
           left stretched

under the wheel—

      suffering the faults

           of timing.

An accident starts

      drying into another

pigment—

      all of the noise

      of witnessing begins

to bubble

      like a simmering liquid

threatening one's

      grasp & then

the quiet creeps back in

as a small collapse,

  dissolving & becoming

a scowl,

a grind/a split—

  glass-broken—

creating an opportunity

  for invective,

snapping

  quiet imbalance

into bluntness

spilling over & then—

  it's finally just.

CAVEATS

Edge of the limit line—

        an admonition/a signal:

the radio arrests—

        disappearances

        & afterthought.

Empty of passenger/

        empty of messenger—

    among
        the yellow star thistle

the ruse drops.

        Rolling back into

the vertiginous curve

of the Earth,

        living shouted down—

something heavenly

        is created—

SHELL

Reveal—
        stretch/crack

open/fall—

sun stains

the skin's parchment

        w/ morning light:

it is breaking/open.

In the shallows,

        newness shakes

& what the air captures

it writes on the skin

        in lists.

Left behind

        is the evidence:

a sheath,

        house of fragile craft,

blood & skin

ruptured,

brought into the cold.

Now dissolved,

        breaking down

into puzzle/myth,

the remnants

        are left behind:

a tongue-tied

coil of rust

        jutting out

an unfolding decay—

still life.

Once pulsing

        stratum & lungs

have become

        other punctuation—

These lines

become a husk—

        this is the opening

of a psalm.

THE EDGE OF IT

Jammed & trapped,

the marine layer,

      sits down

on the head—

creates claustrophobia.

The bones

extend out &

      point crooked—

the day writes

the remainder

of the diary,

terminal messages &

others' distances,

      beautiful demise

on a few lips—

a hushed delivery—

      between cups of coffee:

expectant expiration.

A workplace comedy

is interrupted &

now, spleen blooms w/

special-characters—

      twenty-twenty hindsight.

PLANES

My blindness

under sun's brightness—

      at noon's height:

contrails overhead,

      those minimal

pictures drawn

by vessels w/ vessels—

markers over

the marble's lens.

      These are delusions

        drawn above—

empty w/

loaded questions.

SLEEPER

Remember the fall:

      Nineteen eighty-two

before the morning routine

slumped over

slipped

      into frozen noise

gray bags

      and grimace

bad posture

      breaking ribs

in slow motion

      the small slip

of words:

      the trouble

set back down

      still/just sleeping

an anecdote behind

      glass eyes

      manufactured

laughter too late

slender smile

      while looking on—

the horror show

EXIT SONG

In spy movies:

espionage can begin

        w/ a strand of hair

taped

        to the door—

if the strand is missing

the door

was broken into.

If the door is

        broken out of?

That's different fiction—

it becomes an escape

story/ an evaporation

        of ends/

& afterwards,

        the air becomes

heavy w/

conscience & opinions—

breaking down

        slowly

as impressions

        in a mattress.

It is the disappearance

that matters—

bodies/weight/touch—

leaving stillness

        dividing stillness

save for a few stray notes

        lingering in cruelty.

LEAVING CONVENIENCE

Won't scan/won't sing:

    leftover dictions

tightening flesh,

curling like a suit

    of wood shavings

like doors

    buckling steam

rising

from exhaust fans

placed over

open mouths,

    wakefulness

found in brass rattling

in debate.

Elsewheres start

    trailing off

& the statuary stares

at a season's conflict

conducting

in a chamber of night—

copper edges parting—

fall's opus letting out

        its last notes.

COMEDIAN

Battered into holy arrival

on the stage

      of no stage,

the punch-line

slips out

of the jaw's winch,

screwing up

      into a toy wreck.

It is a line

wrestled from late-night

television—

a thought scuttling

out from under

      restive notes

of urge

unarranged/unrehearsed.

The arriving

solitude afterwards

           is immense—

the joke

is separation, the set-up

in pieces built from

a few clicking

           conversations

w/ lip-sync burn-outs.

The side-door opens &

a fissure   widens

           & w/ the peanut gallery's

banter settling,

the brick dust just floats

a disappointment —

the joke's finished

           before it's started.

RECITAL

Left out after day's ending:

rusted Radio Flyer

punctured football

toy car w/

      cracked pedal

Trembling procession

      until dark,

until the stones

are laid out

In letters torn

into quarters—

      cast out into updrafts—

those battered

      scrawls

depend on only so much

      sunlight

Lines to strange lips

songs crossing/

      left over

ARITHMETIC

The loudest nerve

blooms

into jagged

      flowers &

the structure is

clipped\wedged.

Counting through

      every second

of this calculation—

numbness arrives

but, just below

the surface:

      whips spit,

flickering.

BOXES

split tooth/entangled

busted prayer

      the barely audible

collection of remnants

the dark mouth

      of the garage

captures/boxes

garden shears

      ball peen hammer

drill bits/

photo albums

in patchwork trebles

presiding in

      afternoon light

breaking the windows

left over

the blinking bulb

the act sees

the light fade

        brittle denouement

movie lines—

intrusion

save for the softness

        of a tired bouquet

of unspent goodbyes

the skin finds

sharpness

        in the bark

of a tiny dog

playing sentinel

a figurine

        for emptiness

& prayer in the density

of the lights

growing dim

THE HUM

[*In the transcript:*

an excess of dark rain

on the window sill—a stack of compromises.]

+

Mother says:

It is an invisible string, taut,

pulled from the crown,

a window decoration

against the hum abrasive—

a wooden dancer

        against the abrasive hum.

+

She says:

These are cities of sharp joys,

skies of broken inks,

        skins of sun's sons.

[*In the transcript:*

Save for the rants of a washing machine,

it is an absent-minded, quiet sort of anger

residing in the chapel of the bedroom.]

+

Father says:

It is strung invisibly—

hooked, latched against

the wish bone,

bleached armor,

        diligent w/erosion,

epaulettes cracked

throughout w/ persistence.

+

He says:

These are houses of lovely splinters,

streets of familiar fractures,

        heroes w/ sweet demise.

[*In the transcript:*

Analysis states: the domesticity that swells

in the pipes stems from anxiety & letters

written by grinding teeth together.]

+

Brother says:

The string creates an invisible it,

rigid, narrow around the voice.

It swindles in cup games,

dresses windows for murders,

creates an economy of parlor tricks,

        dressing up violence casually.

+

He says:

These are cinemas

of false divinations,

tortures from possibilities,

        trophies for mantles.

[*In the transcript:*

Under half-buried notions on the shelf

is a diagram of hours/divisions—

plot points & negotiations.]

+

Sister says:

Strung up, it remains

desiccated, a bound up corsage,

a skeleton wearing

           shadows.

+

She says:

These are the gallows

performing,

these terrible instructions—

this weight of the

stain

        that doesn't end.

+

[*In the silence between words where*

only heavy blind-spots exist,

these are love-songs

      that live for attention.]

THE LOVELY RESIDUES

Lingering in the cracks

between fingers—

raconteurs w/the slow scent

of lengua on the sleeves

(a memory of smoldering

picking up irons/

cinders, flaring up—

bringing in ashes/

blessings/songs

half-asleep like a sliver

of moon

tipped over the horizon—

                becoming stories

Adam Stutz is a poet whose work has appeared in *Cultural Society, Prelude, White Stag, A Sharp Piece of Awesome, The Equalizer 2.0.*, and is forthcoming in *Be About It.* When he isn't working as a professional desk jockey, he is co-curating the Non-Standard Lit Reading Series with Mark Wallace. He currently resides in San Diego, CA.

www.ingramcontent.com/pod-product-compliance
Lightning Source LLC
Chambersburg PA
CBHW021454080526
44588CB00009B/845